Zoos keep them safe.

They like to climb trees.

Gorillas sleep in nests.

Some make nests
in trees.
Others sleep
on the ground.

They never use
the same one twice!

Gorillas have lots of fur.

They eat plants.

They love to eat leaves!

They love to play!

Words to Know

fur

nest

Index